I0236414

HUH?
How Living Things Communicate

TALKING INSECTS

Nice spots.

Ditto!

SUSAN SCHADT PRESS
susanschadtpress.com

by Joyce Markovics

Published in the United States of America by Susan Schadt Press
New Orleans, Louisiana

www.susanschadtpress.com

Content Adviser: Dr. Carol Miles, Associate Professor and Undergraduate Studies Director, Department of Biological Sciences, Binghamton University, Binghamton, New York

Book Designer: Ed Morgan
Book Developer: Bowerbird Books

Photo Credits: cover, copyright page, title page, table of contents, 4–5, 6, 7, 9, 10 bottom, 13, 14–15, 16, 18, 19, 22–23, 24 bottom, 25, 26–27, 29, 30, 32, 34, freepik.com; © Mike Redmer/Shutterstock, 8; © Mary Terriberry/ Shutterstock, 10; © Gerry Bishop/Shutterstock, 11; © Margus Vilbas/Shutterstock, 12; © Kuttelvaserova Stuchelova/Shutterstock, 17; © Herman Wong HM/Shutterstock, 20; © Eataru Photographer/Shutterstock, 21; © Holger Kirk/Shutterstock, 24.

Library of Congress Control Number: 2025917917

Printed in China

CONTENTS

Insect Sounds   4

Thank You, Bugs   12

Terrific Treehoppers   18

Crickets and
Grasshoppers, Oh My!   22

Backyard Bug Experiment   28

Glossary   30

Read More   31

Learn More Online   31

Index   32

About the Author   32

INSECT SOUNDS

In fields and forests, flowers bloom. They share their sweet scents. The sun warms the air. Listen carefully. There's a **symphony** of sound. You might hear *buzzes*, *chirps*, *clicks*, *rattles*, and *zips*. Who's making all that noise? Birds and frogs? No. Think smaller, much smaller. These choruses are made up of tiny animals with body armor and six legs. They're clinging to blades of grass, climbing on trees, or hiding in plain sight.

The sounds are coming from—you guessed it— insects! These minibeasts include crickets, cicadas, grasshoppers, katydids, and others. And they're not just singing for fun. The sounds have meaning. The critters are *communicating*. And they have a lot to "talk" about. But what on earth are they saying?

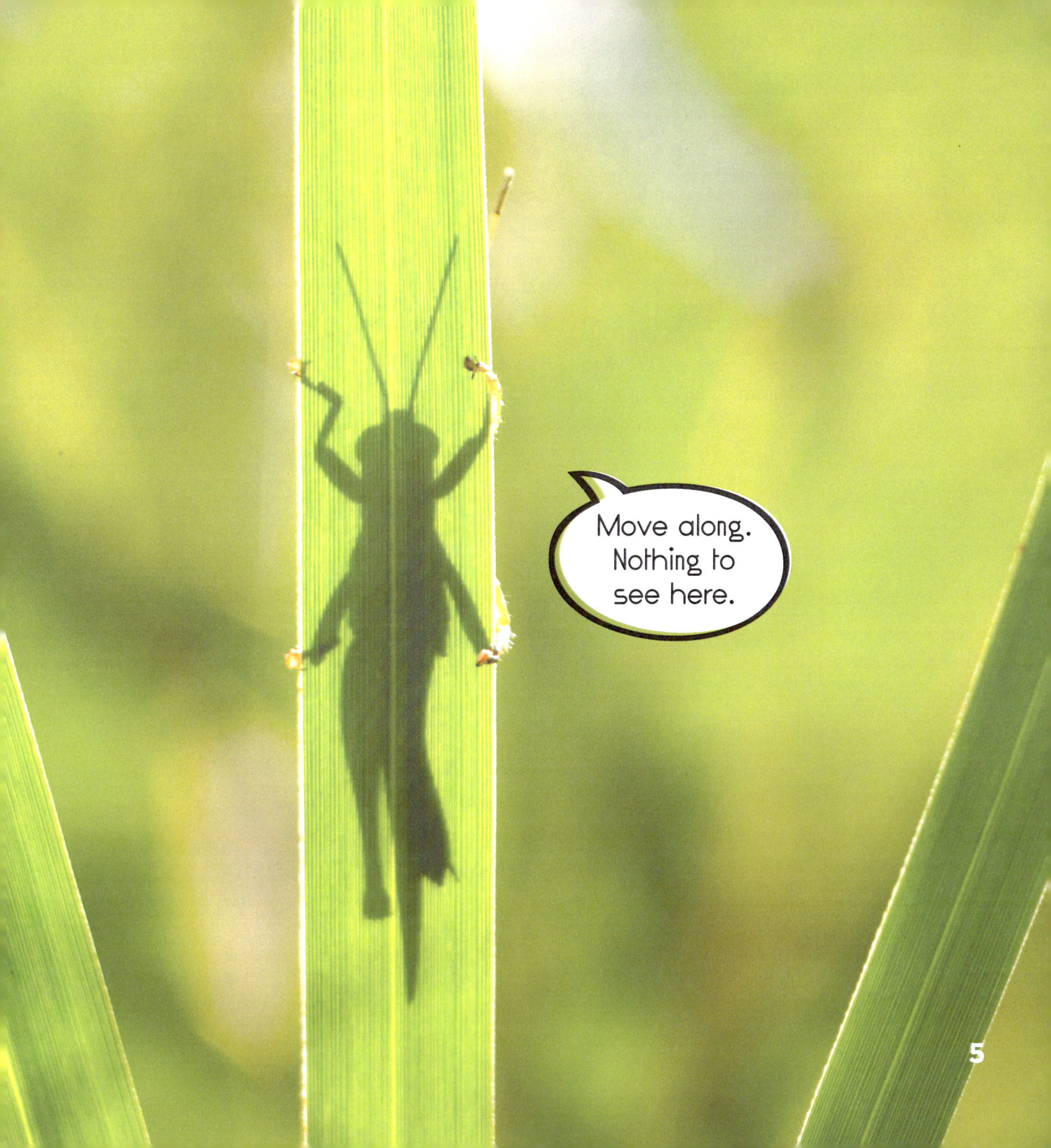
Move along. Nothing to see here.

One way humans communicate is through our voices. First, air from the lungs flows over the **vocal cords**. Then the vocal cords **vibrate**. These vibrations make sounds. Using our mouths, we shape the sounds into our voices. We use our voices to create words and speech. People talk all the time—sometimes too much. It's our way of sharing information.

PSST!

A teacher in England has the loudest human voice on record. It's louder than a jackhammer. Plug your ears, class!

Insects also share information. They don't have vocal cords or voices like humans do. However, some do use sound. And, depending on the **species**, they make sounds in different ways. One of the loudest insect talkers spends most of its life underground. And it's probably older than you are!

A SCREAMING ARMY

In a dark forest, the ground is stirring. After 17 years, billions of red-eyed creatures are wriggling up through the soil. They're an army of periodical (peer-ee-OD-ih-kuhl) cicada **nymphs**. Until this point, the wingless, inch-long insects have been feeding on tree root sap. But it's time to grow up.

There are more than 3,000 known kinds of cicadas and 7 types of periodical cicadas. Here, a 17-year cicada nymph crawls up through the soil.

After the nymphs appear, they march like zombies. They aim for the nearest tree, climb up it, and stake out a spot. Then like a scene from a horror movie, the bugs' bodies crack open. The nymphs are changing into adults! They crawl out of crinkly shells called **exoskeletons**. The new adult cicadas have wings. The bugs are butter-colored and soft. As they dry, their new exoskeletons and wings harden and darken. Now, the scream-fest begins.

An adult cicada dries off next to its old shell.

PSST!

Why do cicadas spend 99 percent of their lives underground? Scientists aren't sure. But some say the insects probably do this to avoid enemies.

BUG BOY BAND

The male cicadas start making loud buzzing and clicking sounds. To do this, they use dome-shaped **organs** on their abdomens. These are called tymbals. And they pop in and out to create the clicks. Air sacs on the cicadas' bodies make the sounds even louder. Groups of males will sometimes sing in **unison**. They form a booming cicada chorus!

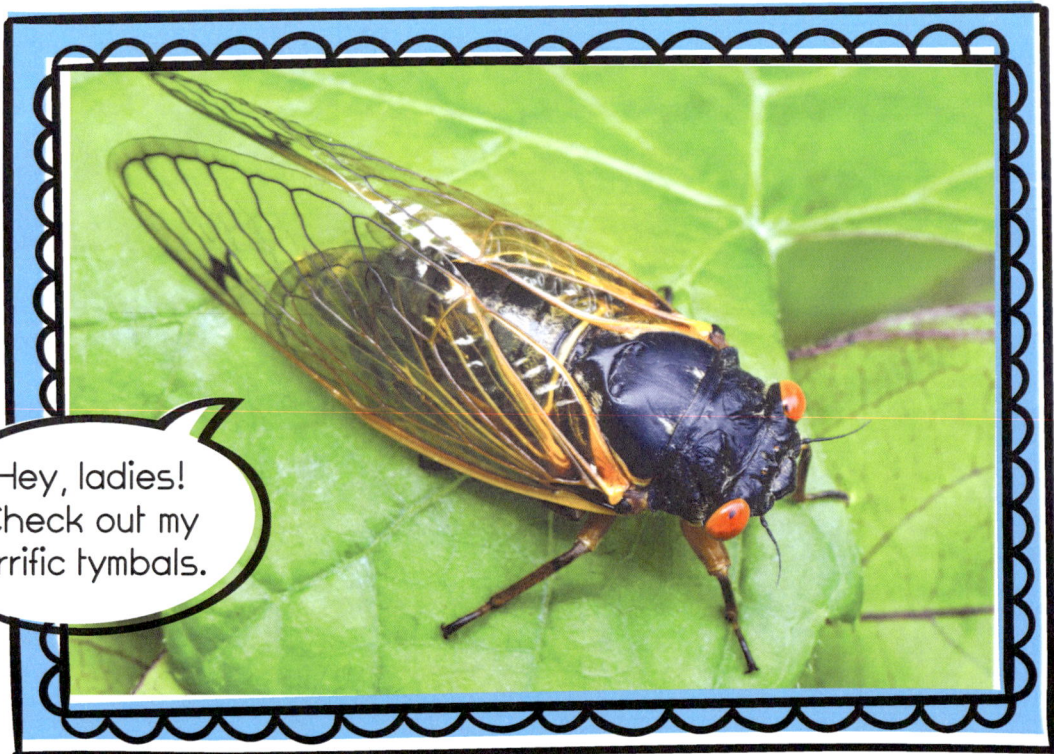

Hey, ladies! Check out my terrific tymbals.

He is so NOT my type!

Same.

Is there a point to the **commotion**? Yes! The male insects are establishing their **territory**. On top of that, they're attracting females. Females, who make much quieter clicking sounds, often mate with the loudest males. After choosing a mate, the females lay up to 600 eggs in the trees. Six to ten weeks later, the eggs hatch. The nymphs fall to the ground where they burrow into the soil. They remain there, in silence, for 17 years.

Adult cicadas die after mating (shown here).
Their eggs look like tiny grains of rice.

PSST!

Cicadas make a distinct distress call when they are caught by a predator. Scientists think this may serve as a warning to other cicadas.

THANK YOU, BUGS

Scientist Samuel "Sammy" Ramsey studies cicadas and other bugs. When he was a kid, he was scared of insects. "It was all the legs, stingers, and weird mouthparts that bite the wrong way," Sammy said. Once he started learning about insects, he was amazed. He discovered that many insects make the world a better place. Some, like ladybugs, control pests. Others break down waste and put **nutrients** back into the soil. (Thank you, Mr. Dung Beetle!) Still others are responsible for **pollination**.

A scientist studies bugs in a field. Insects live everywhere on Earth—even in chilly Antarctica. Picture a butterfly wearing a scarf and six mittens!

Bees are some of the most important pollinators. They help plants make fruits, vegetables, and seeds for us and other animals to eat. Without them, we would have far less food on our tables. Sammy is especially intrigued by bees. "Everything bees do is epic," he said. And, like cicadas, bees make and use sound in fascinating ways.

PSST!

The total weight of all the insects on Earth is about 70 times greater than the total weight of all the people. Now that's a ton o' bugs.

BUZZING BEES

A bee's signature sound is buzzing. How and why do bees buzz? To create this sound, bees beat their tiny wings really, really fast. How fast? Around 200 times per second! To pass on different messages, bees can adjust the speed and **frequency** of their wingbeats. This is important because bees live in a colony with thousands of other bees. The colony is made up of a queen, worker bees, and **drones**. Each has a job, such as laying eggs, finding food, or caring for baby bees. For the colony to run smoothly, the bees need to constantly communicate.

We BEE-long together!

PSST!

Bees don't just use their wings to buzz. They can also make buzzing sounds by moving flight muscles near their wings.

One of the ways bees "talk" to each other is by dancing. "Bees use what's called a waggle dance to communicate," said Sammy. He says every movement "provides vital information to the rest of the hive." This includes where to find the sweetest **nectar** or where to build their next hive. The waggle dance also involves sound.

The waggle dance is a figure-eight pattern that tells other bees the distance, direction, and quality of food.

As the bees dance—or "twerk," as Sammy says—they buzz. Other bees pick up these vibrations, which travel in invisible waves. But not in the way you may think. Bees don't have ears like us. Instead, they and other insects have superfine hairs covering their bodies. These hairs bend when sound waves hit them. Signals are then sent to the bees' brains. Another way that bees hear is through their **antennae**. But the coolest way is through their legs and feet. When a sound wave hits a surface where bees are standing, their legs and feet vibrate!

Can you feel the vibrations?

YES, QUEEN!

Experts like Martin Bencsik study what bee sounds mean. Some of the loudest sounds are made by the queen bee. Not only is she the mother of all the bees in a colony, but she also quacks and toots! To learn more about these noises, Martin listened to and watched 25 hives. Then he compared the results. A queen quacks, or chirps, when she's ready to hatch from her **cell**. After she's hatched and is ready to rule, she toots. Martin thinks tooting tells workers not to let other quacking queens out of their cells. Why? Two or more queens will fight to the death. There's only room for one queen in this hive!

BEE-hive yourselves!

The queen bee (she has the dot on her back) is the largest bee in the colony. And she knows how to toot her own horn!

PSST!

The queen bee produces powerful pheromones (FAIR-uh-mohnz). These chemicals prevent other females from laying eggs and help keep the colony safe.

TERRIFIC TREEHOPPERS

Cicadas and bees aren't the only "talking" insects. Pea-sized treehoppers are another. Some look like bits of leaves or sharp thorns. Others look like aliens! Their disguises help them blend in with the plants on which they live. For little treehoppers, communicating in a big world isn't easy. So, they jiggle their bodies. This movement sends vibrations down through their legs. These vibrations then travel through plants. Other treehoppers pick up these **seismic** sounds. So, what are these insects saying to each other?

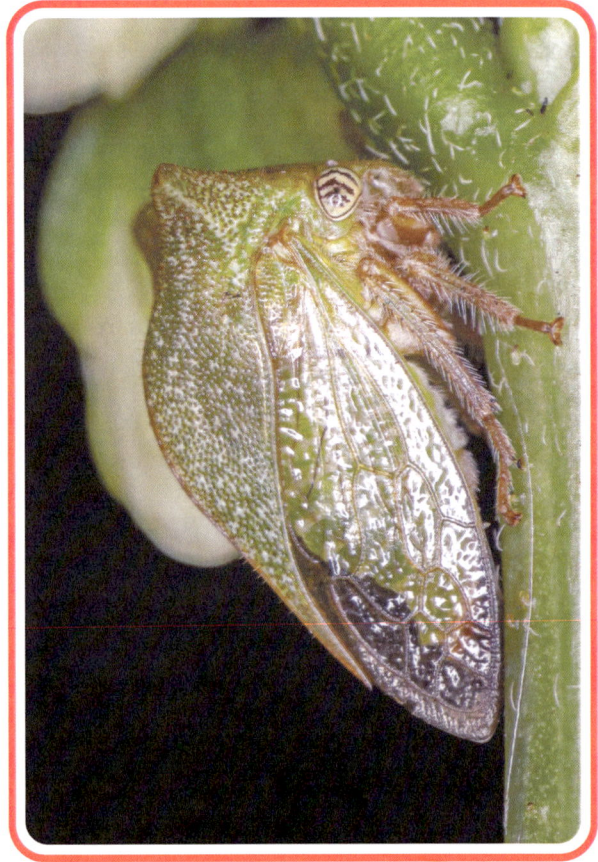

A buffalo treehopper

PSST!

The human ear can't hear treehopper vibrations. So, to capture their sounds, scientists use microphones and speakers. Some of the sounds are "very musical," said treehopper expert Rex Cocroft.

Scientists know, for example, that mother treehoppers use sound to tell their youngsters to stay together. That way, their mother can better protect them from enemies. Scientist Carol Miles wonders whether mother treehoppers may also use clicking sounds to communicate with their babies even before they hatch. Rock-a-bye, baby buggy!

There are 3,000 known treehopper species. They feed on plant sap with their needlelike mouthparts.

GOOD VIBRATIONS

Treehoppers communicate in other ways too. Adults use specific vibrations to find mates. The male jiggles a "Come to me, my love" signal. Then an interested female responds. They'll **duet** until the couple meets up. The love song often attracts other males. Most of the time, the female only has big, bulging eyes for her guy. Then they mate. The female lays her eggs. And the cycle begins again.

Horned treehoppers mating

Scientists like Carol think that treehoppers also communicate about where to find food. And they vibrate to stay safe. If a predator comes along, treehoppers sound an alarm. Sometimes, they call on other species, such as ants, for help. In exchange, the treehoppers offer the ants a sweet, sticky fluid called honeydew. It comes out of the treehoppers' butts. Gross!

Treehoppers have four eyes—two big and two small.

PSST!

Nearly 200,000 insect species use vibrations to communicate, including tiny warty birch caterpillars. They vibrate to tell other caterpillars to get off their leaf!

CRICKETS AND GRASSHOPPERS, OH MY!

You've probably heard crickets at night. They and grasshoppers also use sound to communicate. With their front wings and legs, they chirp and trill. This is called stridulation (strij-uh-LEY-shuhn). Scientist Laurel Symes studies cricket communication. A cricket wing "has a whole bunch of tiny teeth on it," said Laurel. When the cricket scrapes one wing against another wing, sound is created. Imagine running your finger against the teeth on a comb.

PSST!

Crickets, grasshoppers, katydids, and locusts belong to a group of insects called Orthoptera (awr-THOP-ter-uh). They are known for their sound-making abilities.

Crickets don't make as many signals as treehoppers do. But they're great musicians. And great listeners, especially the females. "They've **evolved** to be very, very good at recognizing the exact thing they're looking for," said Laurel. And, for females, that thing is the biggest, strongest male from their species.

23

Just how good are female crickets at finding the right male? Laurel decided to find out. She used a computer to **replicate** the sounds of several male cricket species. Then she played the recordings to two species of females. The first group of females responded to sounds from males from their species. The other lady crickets ignored the chirps. But they went wild for sounds made by their males.

This stretchy body part on a cricket's front legs allows it to hear. It vibrates when sound hits it—like a drum!

Count the number of my chirps in 15 seconds, add 40, and find out the temperature!

GRASSHOPPER TUNES

Grasshoppers are very similar to crickets. But they have their own way of making sound. Grasshoppers have tiny teeth on their legs. They rub their legs on their front wings or sides to produce sound. Sometimes, when grasshoppers take flight, they snap their wings. Each species creates a unique sound—and language. Like crickets, they use sound to find mates and defend their territories. And they can do all this with a brain the size of a pin!

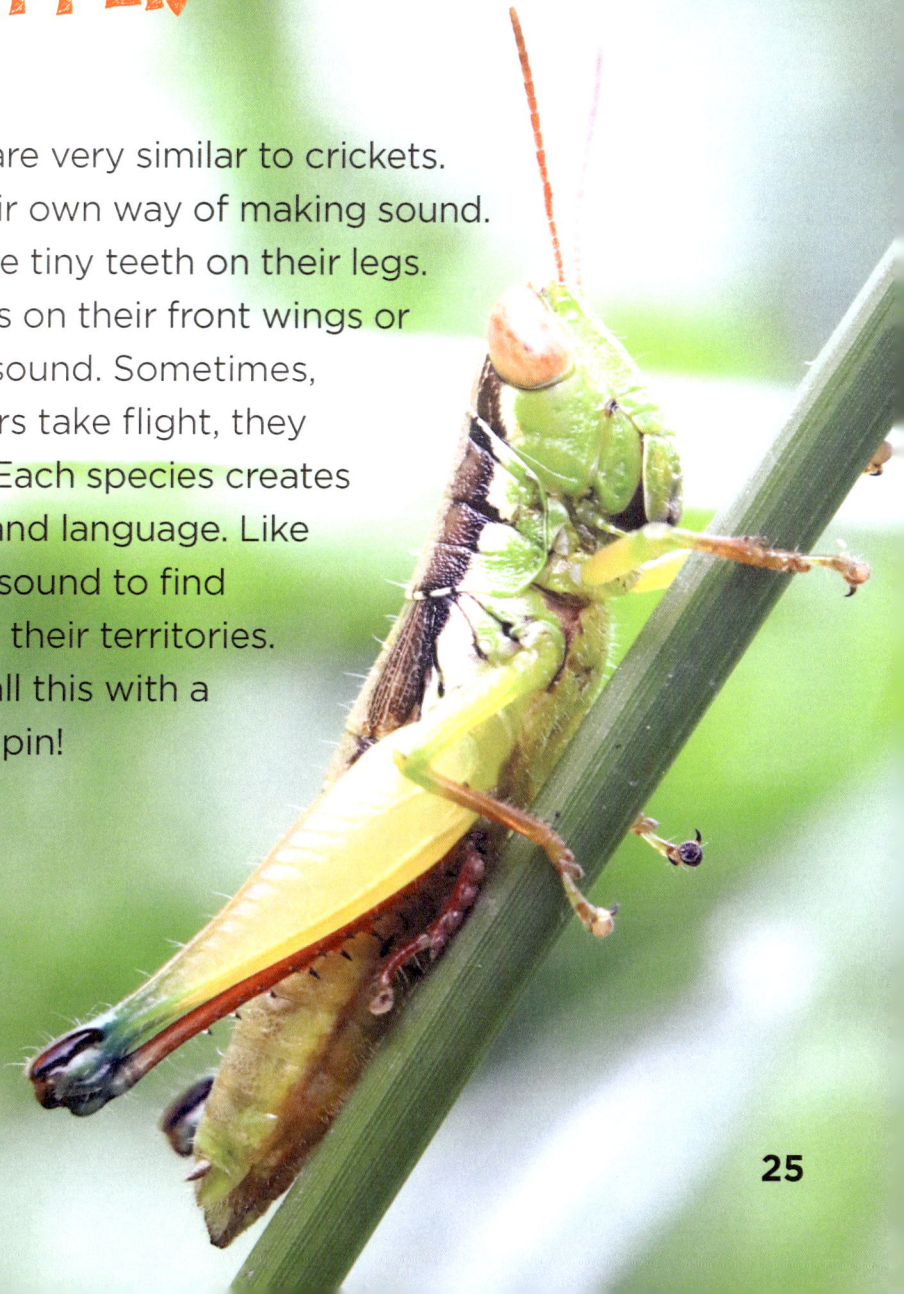

SCRATCHING THE SURFACE

What's unbelievable is up to 80 percent of insect species have yet to be discovered. So, we are only just beginning to identify and understand insect sounds. "We think that we know what's going on out there," Laurel said. "And we're getting this tiny slice of all of the sound in the world."

There's a whole universe that we haven't listened to. By opening our ears and minds, we can learn more about our insect friends. And we can better understand our **environment**—and how to protect it. The environment and all living things are being impacted by climate change, pollution, **deforestation**, and more. So, let's connect—and listen—to "talking" insects. They have a lot to say!

PSST!

Insects have been on this planet for about 480 million years! That's long before dinosaurs started strutting their stuff.

Backyard Bug Experiment

QUESTION:

We know that insects communicate. But can you hear and identify insect sounds in a backyard or park? What do you think the sounds mean? Let's find out!

MATERIALS:
- ☑ Phone or other recording device
- ☑ Timer
- ☑ Paper and pencil or journal

STEPS:

1. Find a quiet spot in a backyard or park. Listen to the sounds around you. Try to identify which ones are made by insects.

2. Place your phone or other recording device near the insect sounds. Hit record and back away.

3. Set your timer for three minutes.

4. Look around. Do you notice any plants or other possible bug habitats that may provide clues about the kinds of insects you might be hearing?

5. After the timer goes off, collect your phone or recording device. Listen to it. Try to identify sounds made by crickets, grasshoppers, or cicadas, for example. Write down your observations.

6. If the recording didn't capture any insect sounds, explore a different area of the yard or park.

7. Listen again and write down your observations. What insect sounds did you hear? What did they sound like?

RESULTS:

Did you hear any insect sounds? Could you identify which insects were making the sounds?

CONCLUSION:

In your experiment, were you able to determine what the insect sounds mean? Did you see other insects nearby? Were they trying to attract mates or protect their territories? Draw a conclusion based on the insects' behaviors.

Shhh! I think this place is bugged!

GLOSSARY

antennae (an-TEN-ee) the two body parts on an insect's head used for feeling and smelling

cell (SEL) a tiny room in a hive used for breeding or raising young

commotion (kuh-MOH-shuhn) a noisy disturbance

deforestation (dee-for-ihst-AY-shun) the process of clearing forests

drones (DROHNZ) male bees whose job it is to mate with the queen

duet (doo-ET) a performance by two living things

environment (en-VYE-ruhn-muhnt) the natural world

evolved (ih-VOLVD) developed gradually over time from something simple to more complex

exoskeletons (eks-oh-SKEL-uh-tuhnz) the hard outer coverings of insects' bodies

frequency (FREE-kwuhn-see) how often something occurs or repeats

nectar (NEK-tur) a sweet liquid made by plants that's collected by some insects such as bees

nutrients (NOO-tree-uhnts) substances needed to grow and stay healthy

nymphs (NIMFS) young insects that change into adults by growing and shedding their shells called exoskeletons

organs (OR-guhnz) body parts that do a particular job

pollination (pol-uh-NAY-shuhn) the spreading of pollen from one flower or plant to another to allow for reproduction

predator (PRED-uh-tur) an animal that hunts other animals for food

replicate (REP-lih-keyt) to copy

seismic (SIZE-mik) relating to vibrations

Did I, or didn't I?

species (SPEE-sheez) a group of living things that have similar characteristics and can have babies together

symphony (SIM-fuh-nee) music that's written for and played by a group of musicians

territory (TER-uh-tor-ee) the area where an animal lives and finds its food

unison (YOO-nuh-suhn) at the same time

vibrate (VYE-brayt) to move up and down or back and forth quickly; when air vibrates, this makes sound

vocal cords (VOH-kuhl KAWRDS) a pair of folds in the upper throat that help humans produce sound

READ MORE

Fliess, Sue. *Cicada Symphony*. Park Ridge, IL: Albert Whitman & Company, 2023.

Manderino, Rea. *The Weird and Wonderful World of Bugs*. Naperville, IL: Callisto Kids, 2020.

Milner, Charlotte. *The Bee Book*. New York: DK Children, 2018.

Ware, Jessica L. *A Day in the Life: Bugs*. New York: Macmillan, 2020.

LEARN MORE ONLINE

Explore these resources with an adult:

California Academy of Sciences: Insect Sounds

Dr. Sammy Ramsey: Your Friendly Neighborhood Entomologist

Natural History Institute: All About Cicadas

Songs of Insects: A Guide to the Voices of Crickets, Katydids, & Cicadas

Understanding Insect Sounds: Nature's Orchestra

INDEX

antennae, 16
backyard bug experiment, 28–29
bee, queen, 14, 17
bees, 14–18
Bencsik, Martin, 17
cicadas, 4, 8–13, 18, 29
Cocroft, Rex, 18
crickets, 4, 22–25, 29
drones, bee, 14
exoskeletons, 9
grasshoppers, 4, 22, 25, 29
humans, 6–7
katydids, 4, 22
mating, 11, 20, 25
Miles, Carol, 19, 21
nymphs, cicada, 8–9, 11

organs, 10
pheromones, 17
plants, 13, 18–19, 28
pollination, 12
Ramsey, Samuel, 12–13, 15–16
sounds, from insects, 4, 6–7, 10–11,
   13–19, 21–22, 24–26, 28–29
Symes, Laurel, 22–24, 26
territories, 11
treehoppers, 18–21, 23
tymbals, 10
vibrations, 6, 16, 18, 20–21
vocal cords, 6–7
waggle dance, bee, 15
warty birch caterpillars, 21

ABOUT THE AUTHOR

Joyce Markovics has written over 500 nonfiction children's books—or at least two giraffe-sized stacks. She's wild about insects, especially the more unusual ones, such as Brazilian treehoppers with their helicopter-like helmets. Telling stories is one of Joyce's greatest passions, and few things are more fascinating to her than the natural world. She lives in historic Ossining, New York, with her favorite human.

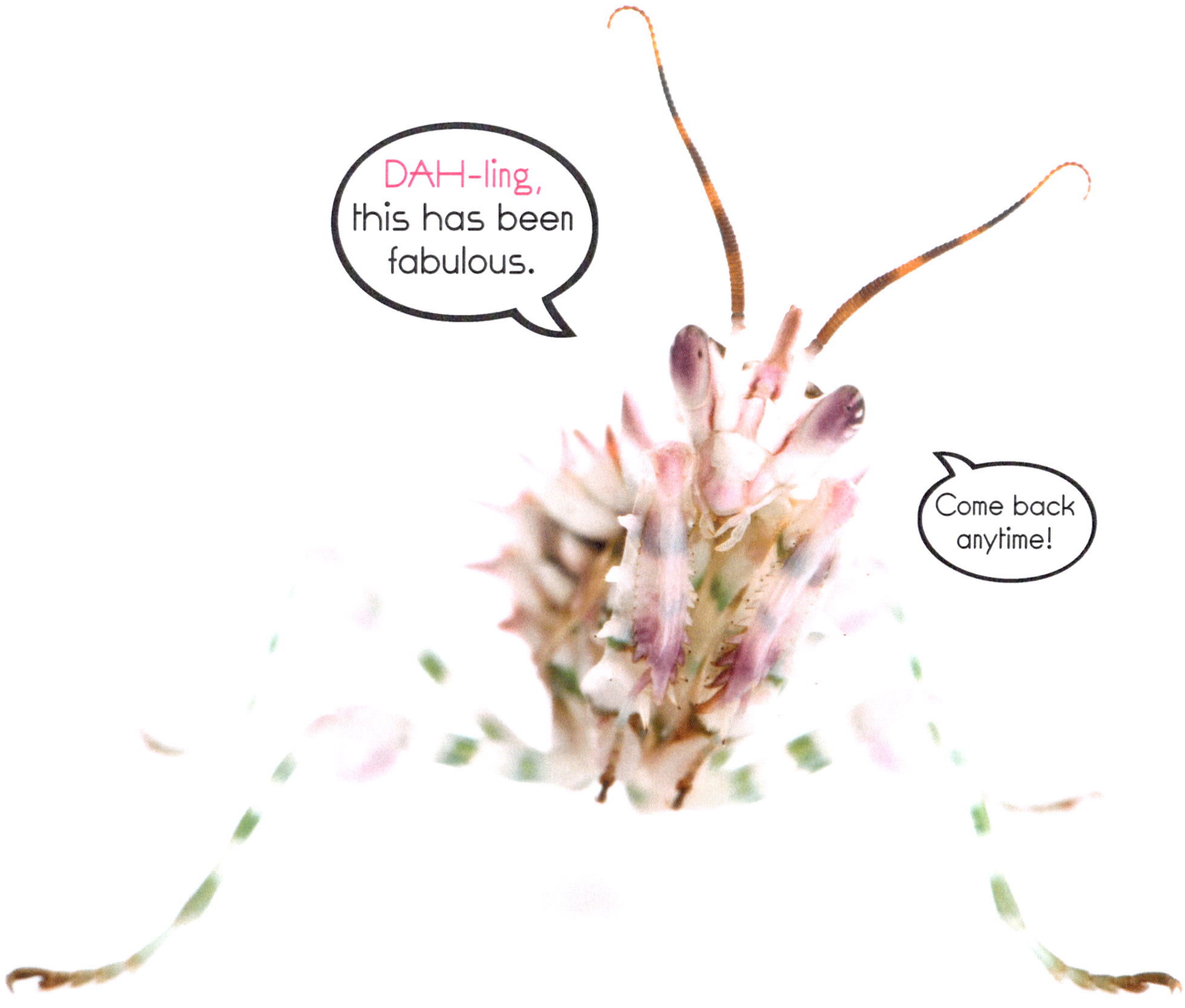
DAH-ling, this has been fabulous.
Come back anytime!

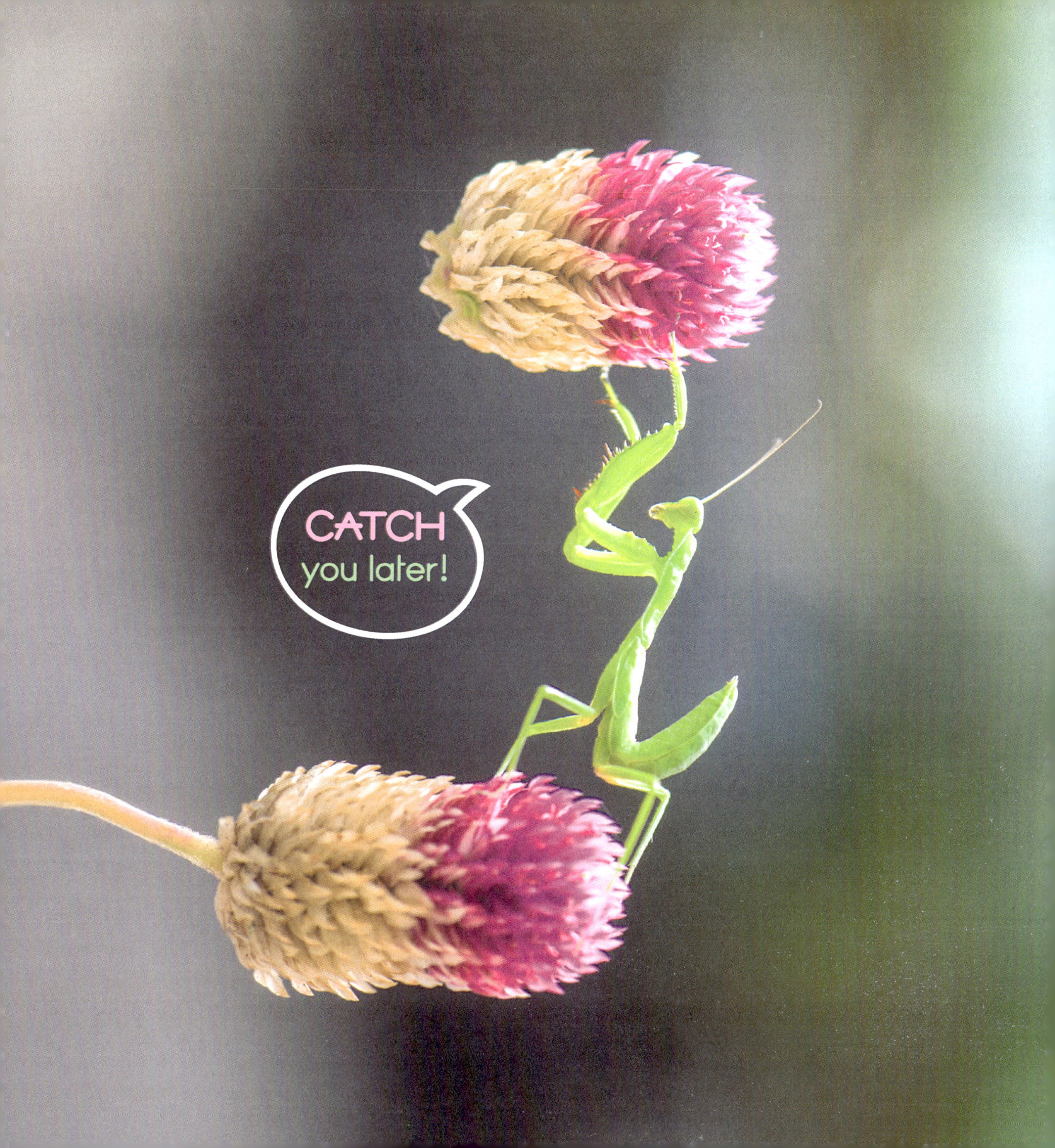
CATCH
you later!